Verses From My Roost

John Ngong Kum Ngong

Langaa Research & Publishing CIG
Mankon, Bamenda

Publisher:
Langaa RPCIG
Langaa Research & Publishing Common Initiative Group
P.O. Box 902 Mankon Bamenda
North West Region
Cameroon
Langaagrp@gmail.com
www.langaa-rpcig.net

Distributed in and outside N. America by African Books Collective
orders@africanbookscollective.com
www.africanbookscollective.com

ISBN-10: 9956-764-02-7

ISBN-13: 978-9956-764-02-0

© John Ngong Kum Ngong 2016

DISCLAIMER
All views expressed in this publication are those of the author and do not
necessarily reflect the views of Langaa RPCIG.

Not for Gain

Multi-faceted God,
I do not ask for much
since my people need more.
Give me just what I need
to keep my wits on guard
in this rushed and wild world.
Give me what will keep me
warm and well deep within
in my roost, fed with light
to light the young to write,
not for gain but for seed.

I look back on my youth
once so soft, warm and bright
with my mum on the watch,
her heart always with me.
I am in love with Verse,
hoping to meet some minds
ready to know my mind.
For now I will stay put
in the dream butcher's fief
to welcome new dreamers,
not for gain but for bond.

Multi-faceted God,
I do not ask for gain
since my people need bread.
Give me just what I need

to keep my kind wised up
in this fast and loose land.
Give me what will move me
move my mates to move on,
on this bumpy playground
I have trodden with care,
not for gain nor for fame.

I look ahead of time
pregnant with misgivings
about the way we think,
bent out of shape, bestial
but give the appearance
of consonance in love.
Give me what it takes Lord
to sow the seeds of trust
in the hearts of my kith,
lost in a sea of sharks
hunting for fame and gain.

At the Game Again

I am at the game again,
playing outside the white box.
I pray those in this great box
do not let fly spears at me.
The wind has no fixed bearing
and air fowls carol their way
into the sky and wide woods.
My songs like running water
well forth in all directions,
refreshing or drowning souls
under the shadow of sharks
that nobody can play with.

Thinking of bruises too much
and the psychopaths next door,
scorches the artist in me.
When the wind of pain blows hard
and the waves of flop hem me,
the poet in me sings better.
The floods of nitpicking tongues
do not make me lose my sleep
nor do disoriented minds
drain the music in my head.
I am at the game again,
hopeful you will play with me.

Writing outside the white box
is a game I like to play,
warm in the arms of the wind.
I will wear no estranged air
nor let my heart outrun Sense
even if Hope flies away
and tongues with teeth tear my songs.
Poets inside the box grey fast,
deprived of sunlight and rain.
I shall cross the great divide
someday on the back of stars,
brighter and more real than dreams.

Fond of Light

I fling words where I want
when the muse slaps my brain,
takes a chair in my heart
and flies me out of flames
to the realm of splendour.
The fields clad in lilies
rise and fall like sea waves
when I stoop to kiss them.

I fling words where I want
but I am fond of light
and love to watch the stars
creep out in an irked sky.
I am sometimes tasteless
but violence I sidestep
to plant subsistence crops
in the hearts of the poor.

I weep and split my sides
in the cold, in the warmth.
I groan while conceiving
music for the grieved heart.
I have fun with the breeze
caressing my stained cheeks
in the heart of labour,
when the sun is asleep.

I fling words where I want
when the muse manures
and blooms make up my bed.
Then I sail in the clouds
and fling away with scorn,
the sword of blind passion.
I will not exchange art
for the tail of a cow.

In The Heart of Palms

Gathered in the heart of palms,
from different parts of the land
with different temperaments,
cloaked in multicoloured gowns,
wordsmiths unroll their goatskins.
Their tongues trumpet their exploits,
frightening away palm birds.
Their hearts eat from Gordian plates,
convinced the world would spot them.

I see them scissor each other,
mantled in the colour of death.
The palms shake their heads open-mouthed
and the sun refuses to smile.
Struck with the lightning of their words,
I crawl furtively toward them.
The conflagration in their eyes
and the rhinos on their foreheads
thrust me into a dark abyss,
hoping to drown my love for song.

The arrows of fear and darkness
plant themselves firmly in my heart.
A mountain stillness grabs my mind
and drags it to a slick window.
I see a multitude of hawks,
highbrowed hawks circling in the sky,
their iron beaks pecking soft brains.

Within the sight of a comma,
the hands of a grand gale shield me
to show me the way to the stars
and how to endure grey critique.

Bag Bright Stars

I have seen many souls fall
like leaves in the dry season,
on the way to carve their names
on the heads of sacred stones.
I feel like a pregnant maid
in the grip of vampires,
struggling in vain to see dawn
and birth a new name foredoomed.

Men used to farm on this soil,
digging their way out of dung
and birds sang blithe in the trees.
Now the land is waste and weird
and the trees too have vanished.
Once in a while a bird sings
but no one listens to it,
no one ventures to see it.

Thinking of the end plagues me
as I walk down a dark path.
Not thinking at all castrates.
I am not without gonads
and my name is with the moon.
I think you can bag bright stars
through the flames and smoke of words,
away from this wraithlike place.

My Balm

When in the bedroom of thought
naked and struck dumb I stand
hearing the voice of Loss taunt,
I sometimes feel my gorge rise.
Poetry, the balm of sick souls
pours liniment on my wounds
and washes out from inside
the dust of bad chemistry.

When the drums of battle beat
in the wasteland of life,
daggers of the mind bring home
chunks of blood in body waste
and body parts on side roads.
Nameless faces debrief me
in the face of rising strife.
Poetry, the balm of sad souls
blooms much in such rotten times.

When the stench of suffering
like the stink of used nappies
drops bombs on my reasoning,
I leave the bedroom mouth zipped
to drink the evening breeze
and spin songs for meliorists.
The world will be sound with them
spinning the wheels of justice.
Poetry, the song for sore souls

is the balm of my temper.

I will not fly to far lands
for the world to take me in
or bring down my cosy roost
for my people to feel me.
I will bid my mind and heart
go to souls with broken dreams
when wolves woo them to silence.
Though time at times has no grace
and birds of prey lurk nearby,
I will phrase on, aware that
poetry is what the world is.

Upholding My Craft

Though vulgarians work me up,
I will not rise to the bait.
Though I am like a candle
flickering in the night wind,
I will not steal someone's thunder.

I hate the art of bluffing
like the fart of a canine.
Frauds love sticking to their guns
like pseudo intellectuals
indignant at pregnant poetry.

I will not corrupt my craft
painting in rainbow colours
the ineptitude of quacks.
They lick up everything bright
like a puppy licks up spilled milk.

Never be green with envy
when you see upstarts ascend.
Let them not get in your hair
nor fling to the flames your pride,
indignant that poets dream a lot.

The Light Grows Grey

Baked in a purple stove,
my songs knock souls over.
They do not turn you on,
flames in the frames of wimps.
You boost only your breed
bred in the school of greed.

Your verses are a flute,
piping the acts of hearts
away from live tight spots.
The unsung name you spurn
to win a nameless prize,
slicing through green raw minds.

I see the light grow grey
in the vault of your dream,
away from the less schooled.
You spend each night and day
tearing the limbs of Art
for greenhorns to hail you.

Seeds sown by a sound mind
sprout and grow near and far.
Bone-dry and damn wet climes
cannot cut short their growth.
I see the light grow grey
in the eyes of your dream.

Tragedy

Crying foul is my undoing,
dashing to pieces like clay pots
the spirit and verve in my songs.
The tight rope of purgatory,
tied to the tree near the river
that bursts its banks every three years,
waits prepared for its next victim.

Let not my thoughts be misconstrued
after the overtaxing years spent
in the inner room of Poetry.
I sing for the silent masses,
those who split timber everyday
for the fires of sacred cows
sunk to the level of demons.

Crying foul is my tragedy,
tearing in shreds like threadbare cloth
the nerve and heart of my verses.
The deep furrows of depression
that run through the subconscious mind,
tell the story of a blue heart
longing to be heard and received.

Hunters

In a sooty corner
in my poorly lit nest
as I weave a new song,
I see men penetrate
the area where I sleep.
With a murderous sigh,
they give my scripts to flames
and pull back in cat rage.

Lone in my deep brown roost,
I give thought to the brutes
and their vitriolic eyes.
They hunt for contraptions
to perforate my eyes,
put a match to my brain
and declare me harmless.
They want to charm their boss
and gain some more medals
before their night grows grey.

I have not lost my spine
in the struggle to trace
the way to people's hearts
before greed screws them up
and the weak of frame swoon.
I offer you their woes
in a time-worn basket.
I offer you their scourge

in glittering grey cars.
They must, to shine better
dash into smithereens
tongues that chop their prestige.

Holding The Torch

Conceit maddens the soul like wine
and beauty like a beast mangles.
Modesty checks the mind like time
and dogs like eyesores indispose.
Imbeciles get under my skin
with politicians wet with sweat,
lost in the woods of their folly.
I almost fell under their spell
to be under the spell of blood
and place a spell on my people.

The endmost portion of my life
stretches before me like a road
leading to the heart of more fights.
I stand like a wave-beaten rock,
thinking of the claws of demons
thrust out to clutch weary victims
and tear them away from the earth.
The spell of enchanting music
cannot make less sharp my promise
to hold the torch for bottom dogs.

Con artists in strangling colours
pour cold water on my poetry
to have me colour their accounts.
I can for certain lend colour
to the story that rats rule men
than to conceit and cattiness.

I may come to blows with self-doubt,
live like a candle in the wind
but will never barter my craft.

Con Artists

The contempt of con artists
and the laughter of madmen,
settle down in my stomach
but do not infect my mind.
I am not constipated.
Con artists can go ahead
and break in bits my pieces.

I have heard of great people
who run through the city nude
to ride the horse of Mammon
and sit on the driver's seat.
I do not begrudge their dreams
even when con artists trill
and raise their works to the skies.

People think I have gone nuts,
cracking the nuts of Reason
to show how vicious man is
and how Silence births hardship.
I do not envy their fancies.
The clangour of their brass gongs
cannot burst my mind's eardrums.

I am not obscured with spleen
as the sun sometimes with clouds.
I will pour out my feelings
like waves breaking on the shore.

I do not fear mouth tigers.
The bells of approaching night
cannot hold my Muse's tongue.

The Hungry Artist

His eyes are ravenous,
his mind omnivorous.
He bites the waning moon
when the inside is bare.
The candle of hope out,
his heart wriggles in mud
near where knackers convene
and the moon blinks aghast.
He wants to penetrate
the deep depths of the heart
and sharpen his cutlass
for the forest of life.

I see him at cockcrow
with cinders on his brows,
sprinting to meet the sun
and shake hands with palm birds.
He wants to fly with them
and make out what they sing.
He wants to wing with them
to find meaning in life.
The days burn like petrol
but he does not flake out
in his innermost self
nor walk like one bereaved.

I hear him in blackness
when the frenzied world sleeps
and the earth groans burdened.
The voice of the night breeze
chants away not for long
melancholy and tears,
inspiring him to sing.
No one approaches him
to gather what he sings,
fighting his way through smoke
to stitch you a green dress
and give us a new name.

Special Day

The sun is red red hot
today my day of birth.
It is a special day.
The wind buffets the dust
and shakes to the core trees.
Weary yellow leaves fall
and branches sigh in pain.
I walk an uncertain path.

Aroused within I watch.
Ego lets go a smile
today my day of birth.
It is a special day
and the dust mounts and mounts
to where Pride lays his head.
My thoughts begin to cough
as I vet the path to take.

The sun is red red hot
today when I am hot.
It is a special day.
I stand by a bruised heart
and the screams of the crowd
in the belly of heat.
I feel grit in my blood,
thinking of thorns and foul play.

In the heat of my thoughts,
the wind kisses my front
and with hands that ensnare
with their smoothness and charm,
carry me to a shade
today the day I prize.
It is a special day.
I walk down a dodgy path.

The Beauty of Self-Discovery

Colourless and desiccated
like packages of shrivelled leaves,
the barbarians of our bad blood
playing the harlot with big guns,
stand in the middle of the road
branching out to self-discovery.

They hate souls that water the land
with tears and unbroken complaints.
They are obtuse and know not that
the beauty in uncovering self,
tears down the wall of gutlessness
and stands up to despotism
nursed by naked nepotism.

They regard with scorn discovery
and the beauty and the grandeur,
the grandeur of uncovering self.
The aura of discovering self
scares them into smoking ganja
from the dawning of dawn to dusk.
I wish my heart could embrace them
to light their way to self-knowledge.

Haemorrhoids

Subjected to all kinds of rape,
the country reeks of haemorrhoids.
Lies shoot up on updraughts of air
like kites fly up high as the sky,
I would that due leaders were here
to pull us from the brink of flop.

Woodpeckers and I day-to-day
race along the unkempt hedgerows
in the conscience of this nation,
pensive and overwhelmed by shame.
I would that able heads were here
to shake people out of their burns.

We labour on amidst dumb folks
to build with words solid bridges
between ignorant and schooled souls
because coming to sense breeds love.
I would that honest hearts were here
to clear the land of haemorrhoids.

On Drips

Sharp-edged rocks of poverty
have thousands of youths driven
into the hands of arse rogues.
Others have fled to countries
they erroneously thought were
greener on the other side,
others have been swallowed
between Morocco and Spain
by a cold gobbling sea.

Tight-arsed shifty Lords of loot
have emptied state treasuries
into the deep of their guts
like the Mediterranean
banqueting on our youths.
Others have stashed away gold
in Swiss and French merchant banks,
giving an indifferent shrug
while the nation is on drips.
They are hard as drawn wires.

Many souls have died like flies
in deep dark wells of hardship,
first fruits to the gods of loot.
Behind lies, their henchmen hide,
hanging around in darkness
to swoop down and snatch a coin
for the upkeep of their offspring

living their future elsewhere
while we crawl through soot to eat.

Longing

I should like to lie down
and wake up with the moon,
wearing a silver smile
in the dew of the morn.
I grow trust in a world
where Justice wears the crown
and Sorrow drowns no soul.
My heart itches for flair
to espouse refreshed mores
and walk along green paths.

A sterling fountainhead
walks tall in my vision.
I see him standing tall
not only with his blood,
but in global bodies
shaking hands in friendship,
speaking of white wildness
flecked with non-white eyebrows.
I will find out his roots
and bid him come to me.

I want to touch his face
and listen to his heart
beat the drum of our lives,
under a grey glum sky
by the edge of a creek.
I want to kiss his feet

and woo his stellar soul
not for boon nor acclaim,
but for the sake of love
sadly scant on our soil.

Lone with Self

I love to sit alone
in this shelter, my heart
each time there is a storm
to view where I will end.

I love to sit alone
far from the noise of shock
each time there is conflict
to converse with the stars.

I love to sit alone
to feel the coalblack hours
I spent scrubbing young minds
to come forth like flowers.

You may erringly think
I have never felt pain.
I have been torn into
and chained in deep darkness.

I will sit lone with Self,
in the shade of my soul
each time you belt my love
to cook the broth of care.

I will sit lone with Self,
far from unhinging tongues
each time there is carnage

to chat with whistling winds.

I will sit lone with Self,
in the bedroom of thought
and give free course to wit
to league with Solitude.

On My Own

I sense I am alone now
on this side of the river,
deep in the mud of life
the stars have put on my head.
I cannot recall the name
my father gave me years back
nor the one I am given
when I cling to what is right.
I want to paint pink my roost.

Yes, I am alone this way
in a box fighting with rats
to see the face of morning.
Do not think you have prevailed
for the sun still wakes me up
and the moon embosoms me
like a plot of garden eggs
embosomed in the forest.
I will paint my roost redwhite.

My desolate heart still sings
in this part of the country,
stark and bereft of honour
amid tongues that hawk contempt.
The kings of the fight within,
those who now down those who fight
those who steal the people's wealth,
hand me their red bag of dreams.
I will hang it in my heart.

Staying Power

Because I find no one true
to unzip my sore heart to
this wild and uncertain night,
I walk into myself stumped.
My feet drag me to a dive
where the poor find fulfilment,
killing bottles of cheap beer.
The stench and fire inside
shove me into the thick night
like a sack of rotten plums.
I have the backbone to stay,
hedged in with folks without heads.

Blanched in the mouth of darkness,
I urge my strong sense of taste
to reach out to the sixth sense
for me to be me again.
The wind whips my eyelashes
and night beetles flute their joy.
I feel the claws of the night
in the skin of my conscience
and weep over my failure
to wing my way to the stars.
I have an elephant skin
to endure murder bites.

Because I find no one fit
to beat the wooden drum with
when darksome clouds fill my sky,

I strap my heart and sit down.
The itch of beating the drum
comes over me like air rage
and my foes hiss in the dark,
The darkling glint of the sky
high-flown like academics
cannot stop me from dreaming.
I have the staying power
to reach my destination.

Soldiering On

You cannot suss me woman
for every time I tumble,
I rise, gather each smashed piece
and soldier on like an ant.
I love to drink from the brook
that ripples and dances rock
through your soft saccharine breasts.
It sharpens my perception.

There is still fire in my eyes
and the voice of longing screams,
scratching the itch in my heart.
I celebrate beauty still
and trek long long distances
to quench the thirst of my mind.
I cannot hold your blank gaze
when blooms bid me to dinner.

I only have fear to fear,
watching the hills wear green suits
when the rains kiss bone-dry Earth
and lick the bowls of dust clean.
I cannot intern my tongue
engrossed in the scent of fame
for you to read me woman.
I only have fear to fear.

The Reason I Think

It is with tears of storm
my beloved with golden feet
that I set foot in your realm
to tack my heart on your breast,
stitched up and down in the dumps
though I am as clear as glass.

Trust me, I am not bloody
though with a wound in my heart.
Let me speak with your small voice
to douse the flames in my blood
and move my blue heart to laugh,
the reason I think I sing.

You are the reason I think
day in day out blown away
beloved beacon in the night,
waiting for the hurricane
with cobblestones in my head
to wrest from tyrants our rights.
I am sick of number two
with a fish bone in my throat.

We have gone through uphill days
aphonic as our raped trees.
We starved for the heart of Truth
my beloved to nurse our dream
and cast our minds on great minds.

This is our very last chance
to stick and stop the bleeding
smudging green red and yellow.

Fighting for You Here

The thought of giving up on you
nurse, twisting your hips back and forth,
struggling to get through a tight door
shakes me like the roar of the sea.
Your silence leaves me high and dry
to take the blame for backing you.

Along in years in this deep life,
I can no longer stand steel strokes
nor bring myself to hail tin gods.
I can, however, face the head
and tell him I hate his headship
letting chaos pee in our eyes.

My down in the dumps kith and I
have lain too long facedown in shit,
counting the cost of bootlicking
besides the price of submission.
We have allowed owls and tapeworms
worm their way to our treasury.

The thought of breaking free of you
mother, in the eye of the storm,
trying hard to shake off our shame,
breaks my resolve to give you up.
I prefer to fight for you here
than from the outskirts of Europe.

I prefer to fall under you
my beautiful wonderful nurse
than under the yoke of green chains.
How glamorous your face would be
like flowers by the riverside
when I lend colour to your woes.

Welcoming Dust

My Love feels faint and forsaken,
my friends assemble in the dark
indignant, bent on leaving me.
My wits drop to their knees nonplussed,
hoping to see the face of Truce
with a tear running down its cheeks.
In the fading light of this life,
I feel the sturdy hand of Fate
squashing my testes like a bug.
Please, do not keep shaved heads for me
or burn daylight with work to do,
thinking you can turn my thinking.

Life's gall has been my companion
since I turned my hand to poetry
but I have kept my head writing.
Life has been merciless with me
digging a deep hole in my mind
to lay eggs of insurrection.
I think I better join the crowd
hammering into shape axe heads
to cut down trees of depression,
hammer out a deal with hard times
and gather all my broken bits,
set for a brand new experience
in the plastic arms of Fancy.

The dust will never reject me
nor the earth vomit on my face.
Morning dew washes clean my feet
every morning when I step out.
A great eagle from the mountain
calls the one in my heart often.
Together they dive down a gorge,
the deep rocky gorge of false steps
and take wing out of it again
to brace their strength in the sunlight.
I will set my spirit to rhyme
with the flames in the eagle's eyes,
certain the dust will welcome me
when the batteries of love run down.

Set Alight Spite

If I can dress your wounds
and open the windows
opening to your heart
my soul will dance reggae.
If you let me probe you
and look into your eyes
wet with the tears of shame,
my heart will embrace you.

Maybe holding your hand
will wake the man in you
view me with pristine eyes
and like coal in the soul,
burn out hatred and fear.
Maybe talking with you
will make the world turn round
to see love in our eyes.

If I can beat the drum
and learn to rise early
to pin my faith on you
men with tongues like needles
will break out in a sweat.
If you can accept me
and set alight your spite,
people will stand in awe.

The world will acclaim us,
the same world that blew up
the bridge of our being.
Let us climb with the moon,
after the dead of night
to light out of darkness
souls still backing break-up
to keep us under thumb.

Sanguine

When you throw stones at me
like a dog with no home
do not think I fear you.
I am a man of poise,
confident like the wind,
graced with brains just like you,
sanguine and neat in thought.

I plump for peace for now
to have done with my work
while the day is still young,
and then fly to the hills
where in the depth of self
the wind and I will merge.
Together we will fight
the monster in your head,
sanguine about our stars.

Like the storm from the sea
we will rise, blow a fuse
and beat down blade hatred.
The state will be more home
than a black hole for us.
The land will be a lea
green, smooth as a mare's tail.
So when you rough me up
do not think I am lame.
I am mad for this land,
sanguine to face the end.

Redwood Heart

I do not recoil from you
as if you were body waste
or the fart of a sick dog.
I detest the obscure schemes,
the dark and deep as night plans
you unwrap year after year
against the wishes of Sense
and the angels around you.

I resent your thinking gear
like the tang from dead flowers
thanks to the steel pipe you smoke,
shipped in from the Hebrides
in secret, obscured with pride.
The mellowing hand of time
may never soften your heart,
hard like African red wood.

I detest my head bowed down
like blooms after heavy rain,
turning over in their minds
like maddened philosophers,
the destiny of people
soft as the soil of a dream.
My mind is a nest of crabs
struggling to understand you.

I must pour out my queer heart
hushed as the grave for so long,
choked by the thorns of envy
and the brambles of distrust.
My screams will fire your blood
and your heart hard as red wood
will burn like coal in my kiln
and heal the wounds of your prey.

Conspiracy

The scheme to skim across
the bay of our being
in the quest of power
my once committed friends,
bores a hole through my heart.
It slits the tongue of Hope,
punctures the lung of Truth
and leaves me deflated.

Unearthly thoughts flood my mind
from the night of betrayal,
the night you drove a dagger
into the heart of the dream
I thought would give us licence
to beat the big drum of love
in our country whole and bright.
There is no lee for turncoats.

Suspicion returns with its fangs
and ominous clouds cram the sky.
Strangers clad in polythene suits
make heavy strides into our fields.
Swallows are displaced one by one
to make room for parrots to pipe
the beauty of darkness in cloaks
and give away our tribe for gold.

The memory of the state lost,
the decision to dream with you
even when the rivers dried up
and cattle lay dead in the fields
wrap their iron hands round my neck.
How terrible to exit from
the house I took years to fashion.
How terrible to be landless.

Staying the Course

How can I hide my face
from the hawk in your eyes
when the god of the mind
and the lord of the heart
judge it right to speak up
for the state to be sound?
I will write what I see.

My head is hurt not cut,
my mind at rest not spent.
My tongue is small not still,
my stance wellborn not mean.
The land needs a sharp head
and a new lease of life.
I will write what I feel.

I stay the course as yet
with those who stand for those
who press lightning change.
In the depths of my heart,
I feel the slur of slight
and the knife scar of threats.
I think I write to right.

I will not hide my face
from the stars in the sky.
I still stand fast and just
to keep the land from beasts.

I will not trade my soul
for a plate of stale shrimps.
I stay the course as yet.

How can I hide my face
from the owl in your voice
when the judge in my head
and the boss of the right
view it just to be just
for the state to shoot up?
I stay the course to teach.

Forlorn Toad

I hear a forlorn toad
croaking in a cracked voice,
outside near a palace
in a freezing cold night,
hunger twisting its arms.
The silhouette of death
emerges from the night
and a clap of thunder
bursts my fragile eardrums.

Trees creak in the night wind
and clap their hands in homage.
Night creatures sick to death
give tongue to their outrage.
Grief slides a new needle
in the heart, contented.
I feel like a pebble
lost in the midst of rocks
celebrating their might.

I am an estranged toad,
choking in a soaked night
near a dark and dank hole
outside in pitch blackness.
An owl declares with zest
its sorrow that I ache
and go to waste unmarked.
At dawn my heart burns out,
croaking in sore protest.

Eyes for Equity

Frustration digs the mind,
the hole deepens daily
and the night of life lingers.
Hatred and betrayal band
and the kiss of death bellies.

I turn in my rare room
and chagrin berates me,
groping for an old horsewhip
for the donkey in my blood.
Grey clouds gather in the sky.

This is my patch of land,
my rightful possession
where the earth drinks in the rain.
I do not have eyes for rule
where souls fall chasing rainbows.

I will not house defeat
nor turn to hole myself
when upon the lap of earth,
naked children cry for milk.
I have eyes for equity.

Training My Thoughts to Rhyme

I brood over moments,
the moments when the sun
shrinks from smiling with me
and the moon disgruntled,
remains in bed all night.
I wrangled with life young
and still do so these days,
my lungs squirming in blood.

I remember the time
a storm moved over me,
rumbling and flashing mad.
It was calm outside though
and children were frisking
without fear, in the dust.
I felt a nameless urge
make a hit with my head.

A storm brews in my breast
and the steel tongue of lies
coin a backbreaking song
I do not fear falling
to kiss the lips of Earth.
I do not fear torture
to unbutton your hearts
and assert who we are.
I train my heart to rhyme
with the thoughts in my head.

I train my thoughts to rhyme
with the heat from the heart
to slay storm, scorn and strife.
I do welcome setbacks
though the storm within me
sparks the need to play dead.
I chew such fate with bouts
on the road to the end.
Sometimes the heart-to-heart
grows dirty and bitter-

Terrible Life

Growing up in adversity
is like a seed shooting up
out of the blue in the wild.
How terrible such life is
like a jumble of jagged rocks
stretching over long distances.

It is hard to come to grips
with upsetting existence
without the finger of God
and the succour of kinsmen.
It is hard to make a name
in a Janus-faced landscape.

Hardship has wrenched at my heart
these many years I have lived,
trying to open it wide
for your sake before I fall.
Nail our colours to the mast
and the world will feel our plight.

Granulate fear, flesh and bone,
grind them well on a boulder
and let the wind do the rest.
Build a fire under you
to appear as night and day
in this dog-eat-dog epoch.

Exceptional Days

On days that wear pullovers
I stay indoors in my shell,
thinking of what will warm me.
On such cold days I write much
on the coldness of man's heart,
hoping that someday a flame
would burst out in his spirit
to light the world to progress.

On such exceptional days
the perfume of flowers fades.
Emotions freeze unfulfilled
and the soul longs for comfort
sought for over these rough years
in the sand and in your eyes.
Unable to kiss the sun
I put buttons on new poems.

Sometimes shadows invite me
for a dance on the podium
raised on the soil of my mind.
Such overtures have sometimes
led me to the heart of woods
where like a spider I hang,
spinning webs to kill hunger.
I will keep my powder dry.

No Flowers to Kiss

In his birthday suit he stands
one more graduate sacrificed
beneath the hairless plum tree
that used to take the edge off
the pain of swallowing shit
to revise his cast and fight.
And the barren fields nearby
where cadaverous goats forage
and their guides bitter than death
dream yet of a better life,
mock their resolve to survive.

A thin sense of belonging
stirs thinly within my heart.
I would that fair play were live
in the hearts of those who lead
to salvage from our old dreams
the spirit of truth and care.
Streams swirl and gurgle with glee
over warm rocks in Freeland
and flowers dance in the wind,
spraying perfume far and wide.
The star-crossed graduate and I
unearth no flowers to kiss.

I try to choke back the tears
bent on standing our ordeal
in the heart of Parliament.

They have reason to feel mad,
sick of the lies and distress
that flourish here like foul weeds.
Politicians have daubed us
the downtrodden with asphalt
to drive through us without pain.
They manipulate small minds
as though they were draughts pieces
and swell on the fear of dons
struggling to kiss dead flowers.

Undraped Corpse

Lain bare at dawn
on twelve bare blocks
in clammy May
next to night soil,
Wung our chief whip
laughs at his corpse
rigid and plain.

Far from eyeshot,
beyond the reach
of our tantrums,
he lies unmoved
merged with the air
to whip our blood
and get us up.

Wung used to weep
watching me sing
with the songbirds
that ignite flames
in darkened skies.
My heart though split
yearns to kiss him.

I will not mourn
not me, the corpse
I see with wounds
from feet to mouth.

I will mourn heads
silent like graves,
to shake our world.

Entrenched

It must not be so.
The people cough blood
in the net of Terror,
entrenched in rocky mounts.
The wind sneezes daily,
grumbling like a waterfall.
I am sure only music,
sweet music can relieve them.

It must not be so,
Rulers do not care
turning men into shades.
The earth awaits them firm,
singing and weaving grey wreaths.
I know the coal of my life
turned to bones, will feed the soil
and excellent crops will sprout,
entrenched behind a tough wall.

The people cough blood,
chained under the earth.
The tyrant cares not
snug in his bulletproof suit.
The writer limns their faces
with compassion and disgust,
entrenched in his moving loom.
The world jumps on his testes,
incensed like a black mamba.
It must not be so noble Head.

Big Gun

He reddens when words cuff him
or slaughter his thraldom dream
in the courtroom of Beauty.
Eaten up with hate and rage,
he robs his closest neighbour
of the nuts that make him breathe.
Worked up, he hovers around
like moths about a candle.

Life and death he tells the world,
depend on his tongue and nod.
I fling away the perfume
from the chest in his darkroom
and watch the boxlike bottle
break into slaying pieces.
In a situation like this,
the portmanteau of self tears.

If I say I can fondle
the strings in his heart with love
in the labyrinth of self,
it is like drowning by choice.
There are deeds deeper than thought
and hearts bloodless and twisted
with hands and feet like talons.
I wish our big gun were warm.

Headache for Doctors

Wounds deep as the ocean,
the headache of doctors
have remained beyond cure
in the deeps of my mind.
A mixture of laughter
at the break of each day
and tears at eventide,
call to mind the lives lost
to keep big guns alive.

You cannot feel my tears
whose hands grope in the dark
nor placate the passion
whose heart longs for freedom.
You cannot see the ruin
lining up like soldiers
waiting for signs to shoot.
Your silence props the king
and puts in the ground seeds
whose seeds poison the earth.

Thistles have taken root
between us, fruits from far.
The earth is indignant
and hatred crows louder
decked out in an outfit
gleaming like the rainbow.
We still can seed flowers

whose petals like diamonds
will not only lure moths
but someday pull fighters
faithful, to free the land.

Victims

The window of my heart
and the door to my soul
are open to fond hearts.
I grieve for souls flown by night
to a cave filled with scorpions,
and pray for friends in the field
at war with their secret selves,
victims of bull-headedness.

The anger in your heart
has taken to mad flames
in the heart of dryness.
I feel blue like a widow,
victim of incorruptness.
I rise at twilight, thoughtful
to climb a hill before noon
because of my honest heart.

Alone on the hill-top
I see the Pale Rider
chewing freshly baked brains.
The sight pierces through the mind
like the lance of a bandit.
Blood trickles out from fresh wounds
and makes its way down the hill.
I watch dumb, victim of scorn.

If dreams near to the heart
and hope set in stone drown,
the pathway home narrows
and beauty dies in the womb.
You need the horns of a bull
to butt the face of Terror.
I will not swim with the tide
nor sail under false colours.

Carnage in the North

In the stillness of the night
safe from the brawls of the day,
my mind gallops to the north
where dark forces draw green blood
from the kernel of the land,
the heart of our commonwealth.
My heart trembles with phobia,
thwarting my attempt to see,
put my finger on the fix
and give the world an account.

There is carnage in the north
under the nose of the law.
The foe decked out for the strike
shoots to break the door closed on him
and cross the bridge to the helm.
His greed has brought ruin and pain
and he loves to grease their lips
with the fat of newborn babes
dashed on the rock of his hate.
I would that foul souls were gone.

We are acquainted with grief
in the south in the forest
deep down inside a rat's nest
where our hearts pulsate in fear.
Our murk and tribulations
like the graveyard's gruesome gloom,

remind me of the anguish
that often crushes the heart
when dreams fail to incubate
and the winds clamour at njght.

It is infernal folly
to be aloof in a fight
that will make life more fitting.
Come let us back the soldiers
that are out to save our dreams.
Tend the rooster inside you
and let it never be late
though its crows annoy spongers.
Affection wants you and I
to stand up and be counted.

Waiting Wet

We have been waiting wet,
the artist and the man
in the pen of sacred sheep,
under a brooding sky.
The naked truth is that
the kingpins of the land
draped in blinding sky blue,
take our silence for love.

Our dream has been ravished
in the backyard of dons
donned in their dusted gowns.
I hear vamps and prophets
discuss late in the night
the fate of our belles-lettres.
I think it must be time
to move ere the earth moans
the loss of her bright blooms.

Wake up seed and branch bro,
stand with me as swordsman
to keep our bloodline whole,
pure and fresh anywhere.
This land we have built on,
this land pregnant with fruits
chokes amidst deadly weeds.
Grab your cutlass brother
whetted well on both sides.
We have waited long, wet.

When Cracks Surface

It so happens my beloved
I shall expire some day
like a driving document,
not in the hands of surgeons
nor in the home of leeches,
not in the shadow of scams
nor in the camp of zombies.
I shall glide across my sky
and go down bright like the sun
when cracks surface and triumph.

The crimson arrows of life
and the beast of bitterness
I thought could be neutralised
taking a trip to Europe,
still splash about in my blood.
So great the pressure today
to cut the ears of Conscience
and smoke the heart of Feeling
when cracks in the skin surface
and the flame of Love flickers.

I see the lantern grow grey
in the winsome home of Hope
peopled with crushed breasts and brains.
The wear and tear I behold
holding their heads in their hands,
open the floodgates to tears.

Before my time bites the dust
you and I should stick like glue
even when cracks do surface.
Hearts with one purpose win wars.

Dream Drifting

The dream was as soft as wool
when I was still growing up,
as bright as a blazing star
the day I turned twenty-five
blithe like a lily in bloom.

The dream turned into darkness
when eagerly, I embraced
bosoms cold and hard as steel
calling the shots as the sun,
fierce as leopards in defeat.

Today, it drifts in the wild
with a lean and hungry look,
looking for wings to sail home
and slit the throat of blue funk
for freedom to stop limping.

Though the statesman meddles much
to please his bloody big gun,
the poet should keep on weaving
and stitching poorly spun songs
to pull hope out of the tomb.

Yesteryear thoughts break open
like a wound that bleeds anew.
I want to quarry the stones
in the mountains of your hearts
and engrave my name on them.

In A Muddle

I do not know who to blame
when the voice of the wind mounts.
All I know is the blue sky
and the dry sore in my heart.
At first I felt no real pain
save the screams of a lone mind,
on the edge of a brown cliff.

A blue bird lands on my head
when the weather wears warm clothes.
I do not know what she brings
but I suppose she means well.
I feel her claws in my hair
and the sore in my soul sighs
but the heart says not a word.

I do not know who to blame
when vision breaks like china.
All I know is the hard life
and the sad moon in my mind.
The day will come when things clear,
when the scales in our eyes fall
and the dead stand up to fight.

The Call of Time

Day in, day out at dusk,
the noise of hungry frogs
drills a hole in my mind,
The thought of missing out
on the dance in the rains
throws a spear at my heart
and the call of time haunts.

Where do I go from here
with twelve pins in my heart?
Where do I go from here
without thorns in my flesh?
The memory of dried dreams
shakes the frame of my life
and the call of time grinds.

I hear the call of time
in my soul doleful, mute
despite the rains and wind
whispering hope, certain
to find me on my feet,
fondling a newborn song.
The call of time persists.

Where do I gallop to
where people can hug me
and line my lines with silk?
Here dreams are worn-jeans

flung aside to be burnt.
My nerves are still intact
though the call of time socks.

The Night Closes In

The hills around me are gleeful,
as gleeful as a pig in shit.
They are neither greedy nor bent
like human beings with sick minds.
There is no pain in man's life
as galling as being brushed off
defending the soul of Justice.

To live dry and bare as a stone
is a great burden to the mind.
The soul enchained in a sand pit
breaks out once in the dry season.
Lame rulers flip on bullfrog smiles
bent on feeding fatter their greed
to the detriment of justice.

The night is closing in on me
under scourges, my free will bound.
I have spoken to you in verse
about the shame we wear daily,
hoping you will carry afar
the pollen grains of our mindset
that our heritage may not sink.

The night is closing in on me
under the scourge of my small voice.
I think we should bestir our brains
and season our flesh with spice meet

in this stiff to break through terrain.
The root of shame will decay soon
so I choose to deride the night.

Soon the End

The end will come soon
and sham stars will sink.
I see them from here
in line with the moon,
haloed in ground clouds.
I hear them quibbling,
falling from their Lord's grace,
fear in their hate eyes.

The end will come soon
and we all will fall.
The rich and the poor
the young and the old
the weak and the strong
the small and the great
the dull and the bright
the foul and the cute
the true and the false,
shall be food for worms.

There is no soul sane
nor mind in this place
that can spin a song
in your favour Sham,
no heart to kiss you
 nor friend and caller
to ease your distress.
Leech-like you hang on

to the back of Brawn,
watching the state die.
The end will come soon
and tin gods will fall.

Worrying

My dearly loved Motherland
raped a million and one times
in the light by your own children
and in darkness by strange Cats.
I see only grey grey skies
and whips and chains in your silence.

The tongues of politicians
slippy as they are end up
leading souls down a slippery slope.
The hungry so deep in drought
tear each other's dry throats out
to see the light of tomorrow.
Your silence beloved, scrapes the mind.

I do not know how you feel
when all around you is dark
and dreams fade away like a cloud.
The consuming flame of spleen
burns each line of the love poems
I wrote to bask in your favour.
Better to bleat and show the world
the blood on your yellow garments.

Mend or Bow

The thoughts of politicians
crooked as they are end up
baiting with yayin the naive.
The dying so deep in debt
curse the living for bad faith
since the leadership endorsed crime.

The time is coming says Earth
when every blank tree will fall.
There will be no hiding enclave,
no sympathy for the bent.
Believe me aspiring smith,
there will be no more Brutuses.

We have descended too low
in the court of the world
crouching in bruising ignorance,
waiting to rise to the bait
in the guile of grey honchos.
Mend your rule dear heads or bow out.

The time is coming says Time
when every dream and dogma
will melt like wax in the sun.
There will be no time for creeps
to win the favour of kings.
Mend your ways folks and bow to be.

Printed in the United States
By Bookmasters